Welcome to
Computers for
ESL Students,
2nd Edition
Workbook:
Windows XP Version

OLIVIA ADENDORFF
Manteca Adult School

LOIS WOODEN
Manteca Adult School

LABYRINTH
L E A R N I N G ®

President:
Brian Favro

Acquisitions Editor:
Jason Favro

Managing Editor:
Laura A. Lionello

Production Manager:
Rad Proctor

Editorial/Production Team:
Belinda Breyer, Arl Nadel, Sheryl Trittin

Cover Design:
Huckdesign

LABYRINTH
L E A R N I N G ®

Welcome to Computers for ESL Students, 2nd Edition Workbook: Windows XP Version
by Olivia Adendorff and Lois Wooden

Copyright © 2009 by Labyrinth Learning

Labyrinth Learning
P.O. Box 20818
El Sobrante, California 94820
800.522.9746
On the web at www.lablearning.com

ITEM: 1-59136-197-4
ISBN-13: 978-1-59136-197-8

Manufactured in the United States of America.

0 9 8 7 6 5 4

Table of Contents

Learning About Computer Basics

WORKBOOK 1.1 Fill in the Blanks

Write the name of each item that the arrow is pointing to.

Figure coourtesy of 123RF™

1. _____

2. _____

3. _____

4. _____

5. _____

With a partner, take turns reading the A and B parts of the conversation. Fill in each blank with the right word (or words) from the Word Bank.

WORD BANK

computer	exciting	CPU	brain	monitor
screen	keyboard	keyboarding	mouse	buttons
push	turn on	power button	Desktop	computer

Student A	Hi. What's that?	
Student B	This is my new _____.	
Student A	Really? How _____!	
Student B	Let me show you. This is the _____.	
Student A	I know. It's the _____.	
Student B	That's right! This is the _____.	
Student A	Wow! It has a nice _____.	
Student B	I know. This is called the _____.	
Student A	Yeah, I know that word. My brother takes _____ at school.	
Student B	This is the _____ and these are the mouse _____.	
Student A	What a cute mouse. Can I _____ the button?	
Student B	Not yet! You have to _____ the computer first.	
Student A	OK. Can I push the _____ to turn it on now?	
Student B	Sure. The first thing you see is the _____.	
Student A	The colors look good.	
Student B	I know. I love my new _____!	
Student A	You are so lucky!	

Vocabulary Worksheet

Fill in the blanks. Select the best answer for each sentence, using the vocabulary words in the Word Bank.

WORD BANK

CPU	Desktop	icon
keyboard	monitor	mouse
mouse button	power button	screen

1. To turn on the computer, press the _____.

2. You type on the _____. It has letters, symbols, and functions.

3. An _____ is a picture that represents a program or a command.

4. A _____ is the part of the computer system that includes the screen and its controls.

5. The _____ is the part of the computer that lights up and shows what is happening on the computer.

6. The _____ is the first thing you see on your screen when you turn on your computer.

7. To "click" means to press the _____.

8. The _____ lets you point to different things on the computer screen.

9. The _____ is where all the "thinking" in the computer is done.

Verb Worksheet

Fill in the blanks. Select the best answer for each sentence using the computer verbs in the Word Bank.

WORD BANK

turn on	turn off	go to
press	let go	shut down
click	drag	select

1. To _____ the computer means to turn it off by using the Start menu.

2. Before you can use a computer, you must _____ the CPU and the monitor.

3. To press and let go of the mouse button in one smooth motion is called to _____.

4. To _____ means to take your finger off the mouse button after you press it.

5. When you choose something in particular, you _____ it.

6. To turn on your computer, you have to _____ the power button.

7. When you are finished using the computer, you should _____ the computer.

8. When you want to move something to a different position on the screen, you can _____ it with your mouse.

9. To _____ means to take your mouse pointer to a place on your screen.

Fill in the Blanks

Write the name of each item that the arrow is pointing to.

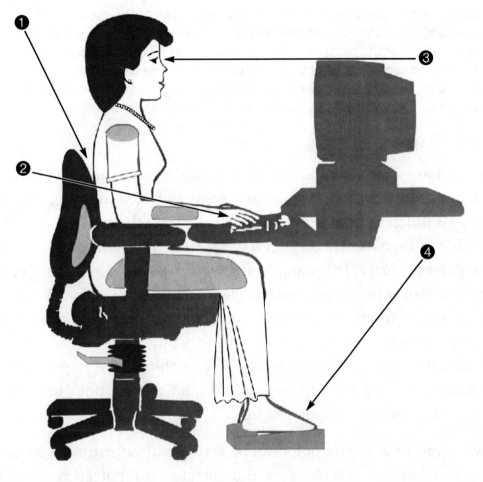

1. Sit up _____ in your chair.

2. Keep your _____ straight.

3. The top of the monitor should be at the same level as your

   _____.

4. Sit with your _____ flat on the floor.

PARTNER PRACTICE

After you fill in the blanks correctly, close your book. Without looking at your book, tell a partner the four sitting positions that are important for working at the computer properly. You and your partner should take turns telling each other the four important sitting positions.

Partner Activity: Practice Reading and Pronunciation

Your teacher will read the paragraphs below as you listen to the pronunciation. Then, with a partner, take turns reading the paragraphs for one minute. The listening partner will circle words that the reader needs to practice pronouncing. Alternate reading, and listening and circling words with your partner. If you get to the end of the paragraphs before the minute ends, begin reading at the beginning. Each partner should practice reading two or three times. Ask your teacher for assistance, as needed.

PRACTICE READING

Learning how to use a computer can be difficult, but it can also be a lot of fun. You have to learn new vocabulary words and their meanings. Computer language is different from everyday language. Sometimes words that mean something in everyday language can mean something completely different in computer language. For example, the word "mouse" has a completely different meaning in computer language than it does in everyday language. Working with equipment can also be challenging. Some people can work with equipment very easily, but it may be very difficult for others. Everybody has different levels of ability at doing different things. The important thing to remember is to try, try, and try again. You have to continue to learn, understand, improve, and not give up!

Knowing how to use a computer can be very useful. Sometimes you can't get a job if you don't know how to use and operate a computer. Computers are everywhere these days, and it's important to be able to use them. Children are now learning how to use computers in elementary school. They learn how to use computers much faster and easier than adults do. Adults need to keep up with what their children are learning at school. Sometimes adults may also have to monitor what their children do with computers and learn how to best help and protect them.

What I Have Learned

Take some time to think about what you have learned in Lesson 1. With a partner, take turns asking each other the questions in Exercise A and discussing the topics in Exercise B below.

EXERCISE A

Ask your partner the questions below. Begin each question with "Did you learn…." Your partner's answer should either be "Yes, I did" or "No, I didn't." Circle the answer that your partner provides.

"Did you learn…"		
• Different things you can do with a computer?	Yes	No
• To turn the computer on and off?	Yes	No
• To identify the major parts of the computer?	Yes	No
• The difference between a CPU and a monitor?	Yes	No
• The difference between a concept and an exercise?	Yes	No
• The different parts of the mouse?	Yes	No
• How to place your hand on the mouse?	Yes	No
• How to move the mouse pointer?	Yes	No
• How to drag icons?	Yes	No

When both you and your partner have finished asking and answering the questions, look at the "No" answers on your sheet. Study and practice your book some more. Continue asking each other these questions until both of you can answer "Yes" to all of the questions.

EXERCISE B

Talk about the topics below with your partner. Do you agree or disagree with your partner? Discuss your responses.

• Name two different parts of the computer.

• Tell me the difference between a monitor and a screen.

• Describe the correct way to sit at a computer.

• Tell me how to turn off the computer.

Crossword Puzzle

Fill in the words across and down to complete the puzzle.

ACROSS

3. To press and let go of the mouse button (left side) in one smooth motion

5. To push a button with your finger

8. To take your mouse pointer to a place or a program that you see on your screen

9. The small oval piece that you can use to move from one part of the screen to another

10. The part of the monitor that lights up and shows what is happening on the computer

12. To use your mouse to take something to a different position

13. To turn off the computer using the Start menu

14. The part at the top of the mouse (left side) that you use to control the mouse

15. To give power to the computer so that it works

DOWN

1. The brain of the computer system

2. The part that you type on, which has all of the letters, symbols, and functions

4. To take your finger off the mouse button after you press it

6. The button that turns on the computer

7. The first thing you see on your screen when you turn on the computer

9. The part of the computer that you look at to see your work; like a television

11. A picture that represents a program or a command

13. To choose a letter, word, sentence, paragraph, or program

Using Windows and the Start Menu

WORKBOOK 2.1 **Fill in the Blanks**

Write the correct word to describe each part of the Windows Desktop.

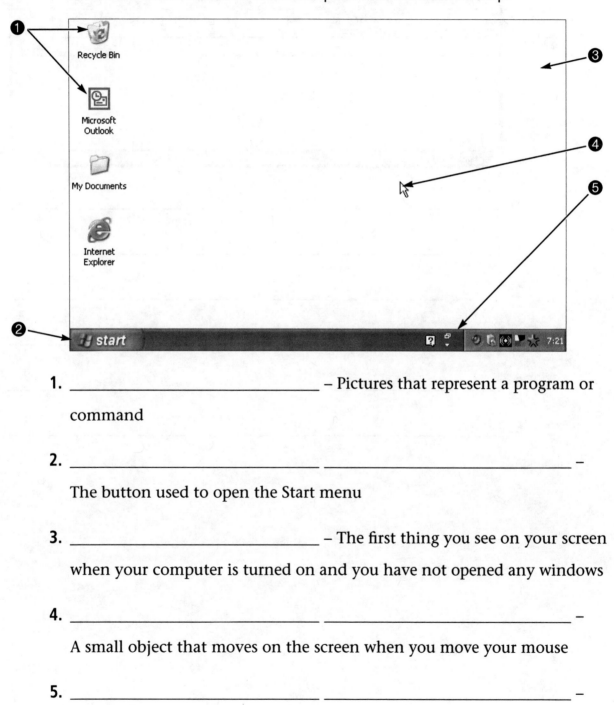

1. _____ – Pictures that represent a program or

command

2. _____ _____ –

The button used to open the Start menu

3. _____ – The first thing you see on your screen

when your computer is turned on and you have not opened any windows

4. _____ _____ –

A small object that moves on the screen when you move your mouse

5. _____ _____ –

The bar at the very bottom of the screen. It shows all open programs

WORKBOOK 2.2 **Fill in the Blanks**

Write the name of each item that the arrow is pointing to.

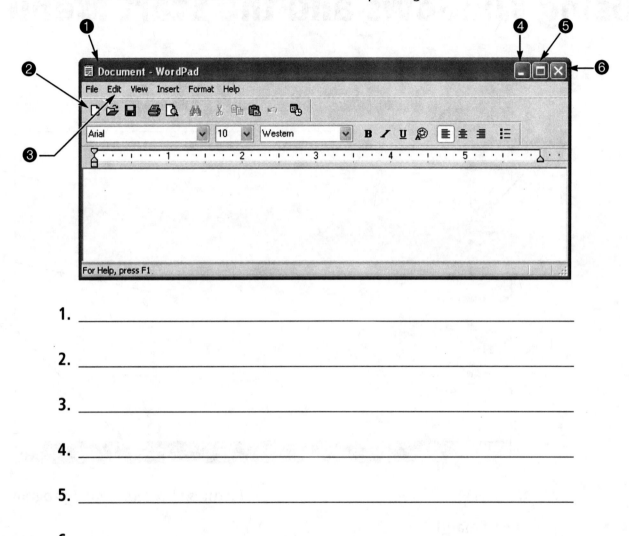

1. _____

2. _____

3. _____

4. _____

5. _____

6. _____

WORKBOOK 2.3 **Paired Conversation**

With a partner, take turns reading the A and B parts of the conversation. Fill in each blank using the vocabulary words and computer verbs in the Word Bank.

WORD BANK

close	open	screen	computer	window
Start button	Start menu	title bar	menu bar	toolbar

Student A	Good morning.
Student B	Hi. What are we studying today?
Student A	I think we are going to learn how to open and _____ a window.
Student B	Do you mean if the temperature gets too hot in here?
Student A	No! I mean to _____ a window on our computers.
Student B	My computer doesn't have any windows. It only has a _____.
Student A	Don't be silly! There are windows inside your _____.
Student B	Oh! How do you open a _____?
Student A	Well, we will learn that today.
Student B	Will we have to use the _____?
Student A	Yes, and the _____ too.
Student B	That will be interesting.
Student A	We'll learn about different parts of a window.
Student B	I know about the _____.
Student A	That's great. You'll learn about the _____, too.
Student B	What else is important to learn?
Student A	Well, the _____ tells you what tools you can use.
Student B	I can't wait to start!

Vocabulary Worksheet

Fill in the blanks. Select the best answer for each sentence using vocabulary words in the Word Bank.

WORD BANK

window	Close button	title bar
Minimize button	Maximize button	Start button
Start menu	Restore button	task bar
menu bar	program	toolbar

1. The square button between Minimize and Close that makes your window fill the whole screen is called the _____.

2. The button that opens the Start menu and is on the bottom-left corner of your screen is the _____.

3. The bar at the bottom of the screen that shows all open programs is called the _____.

4. A rectangular area on the screen that shows a program or message is called a _____.

5. The _____ has different icons. Each icon does a different job when you click on it.

6. This button looks like a minus sign. It makes the window disappear, but the program is still open. It is called the _____.

7. The _____ shows when you click on the Start button. It lists the main programs.

8. The button with an "x" that makes the window disappear and closes the program is the _____.

9. The button in the same place as Maximize that changes a maximized window to a smaller size is the _____.

10. The _____ is below the title bar. It gives you choices for using the program.

11. The very top of a window that shows the name of the program you are using is called the _____.

12. A _____ is a set of directions that tells the computer what to do to get a job done.

Verb Worksheet

Fill in the blanks. Select the best answer for each sentence using the computer verbs in the Word Bank.

WORD BANK

open	point	minimize
restore	maximize	close

1. To _____ means to make the window larger so it fills the entire screen.

2. To show a window, you have to _____ it.

3. To _____ means to change a maximized window to a smaller size.

4. To make the mouse pointer go over something that you want to choose is called to _____.

5. To keep a window open but make it disappear so that only its button shows on the task bar is to _____ the window.

6. To stop a program so that it does not show on your screen is to _____ it.

Fill in the Blanks

Look at the directions below for opening and closing the Notepad window. You have already done this exercise in the Skill Builder part of your book. Try to remember how to do this exercise and fill in the blanks to properly open and close the Notepad window.

1. Open Notepad: Click _____, then

_____, then _____,

then _____.

2. Find the title bar.

3. Find the _____ 🔲,

_____ 🔲, and

_____ ❌ buttons.

4. Click the _____ button to make the Notepad

window fill the screen. It turns into the 🔲

_____ button.

5. Click the Restore button to make the window smaller again.

6. Click the 🔲 _____ button.

7. Click the 🔲 Untitled - Notepad button on the taskbar to restore the window.

8. Put your mouse pointer on the _____ to move

the Notepad window to different places on the Desktop.

Partner Activity: Practice Reading and Pronunciation

Your teacher will read the paragraphs below as you listen to the pronunciation. Then, with a partner, take turns reading the paragraphs for one minute. The listening partner will circle words that the reader needs to practice pronouncing. Alternate reading, and listening and circling words with your partner. If you get to the end of the paragraphs before the minute ends, begin reading at the beginning. Each partner should practice reading two or three times. Ask your teacher for assistance, as needed.

PRACTICE READING

Learning to work with the Windows Desktop is a very important process. You have to learn about the icons and how to recognize each icon so you know which one to use. You have to be able to use the Start button so you can open and use the Start menu. It is important to practice moving the mouse and watching the mouse pointer move on the Desktop so you can manage it. The taskbar at the bottom of the screen shows you all of the open programs. This is also very useful. Actually, it shouldn't take very long to become familiar with the Windows Desktop. If you are patient and concentrate on what you are doing, you may realize that it will become familiar to you in a short time.

Working with the WordPad program can be a lot of fun. You can find the program by clicking the Start button, moving your mouse to the All Programs menu, then to the Accessories menu, and then finally clicking on WordPad. When WordPad opens, you will see the title bar at the very top of the window. It tells you the name of the program you are using. You will also see the menu bar and some toolbars. There are three window sizing buttons that you use very often. The Minimize button makes the window disappear. The Maximize button makes the window fill the whole screen. The Restore button makes the window return to the size it was before it was maximized. It shares the same button with the Maximize button, but it shows two little boxes inside the button. The Close button closes the window and the program.

What I Have Learned

Take some time to think about what you have learned in Lesson 2. With a partner, take turns asking each other the questions in Exercise A and discussing the topics in Exercise B below.

EXERCISE A

Ask your partner the questions below. Begin each question with "Can you...."
Your partner's answer should either be "Yes, I can" or "No, I can't." Circle the answer that your partner provides.

"Can you..."		
• Find the Start button?	Yes	No
• Identify the taskbar?	Yes	No
• Find the Accessories menu?	Yes	No
• Open and close WordPad?	Yes	No
• Identify the title bar in WordPad?	Yes	No
• Use the window sizing buttons?	Yes	No
• Find the Restore button?	Yes	No
• Move a window?	Yes	No

When both you and your partner have finished asking and answering the questions, look at the "No" answers on your sheet. Study and practice your book some more. Continue asking each other these questions until both of you can answer "Yes" to all of the questions.

EXERCISE B

Talk about the topics below with your partner. Do you agree or disagree with your partner? Discuss your responses.

• Name two parts of the Windows Desktop.

• Name two parts of a program window.

• Name two window sizing buttons.

• Where do you put your mouse pointer to move a window?

• Describe the Close button.

• How do you find the Calculator program?

Fill in the words across and down to complete the puzzle.

ACROSS

1. A set of directions that tells the computer what to do to get a job done

3. To stop a program

5. To show a window

7. To change a maximized window to a smaller size

8. The button that looks like a minus sign on the top-right of a window

11. A bar showing different icons that each do a different job

13. A rectangular area on the screen that shows a program or message

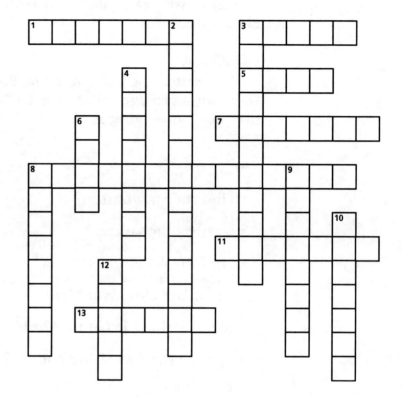

DOWN

2. The square button between Minimize and Close that makes a window fill the whole screen

3. The button with an "x" that closes the window

4. To make a window disappear (but not close) so that only its button shows on the taskbar

6. The bar with words on it that is below the title bar

8. To make the window larger so that it fills the entire screen

9. The bar at the top of a window that shows the name of the program you are using

10. The bar at the bottom of the screen that shows all open programs

12. To make the mouse pointer touch something that you want to choose

Using Windows Programs

WORKBOOK 3.1 **Fill in the Blanks**

Write the correct word that goes in each blank.

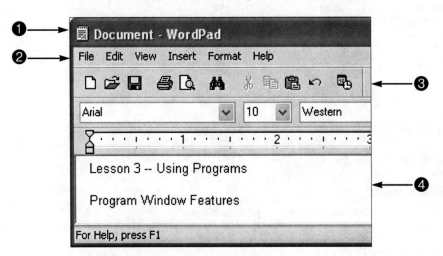

The WordPad Program Window

1. _____ _____

tells you what program you are using.

2. _____ _____

lists commands that let you do different things to your work.

3. The _____ has icons that do different things

when you click them.

4. The _____ _____

is the place where your work shows when you put it in by typing or using

the mouse.

Fill in the Blanks

Write the correct word that goes in each blank.

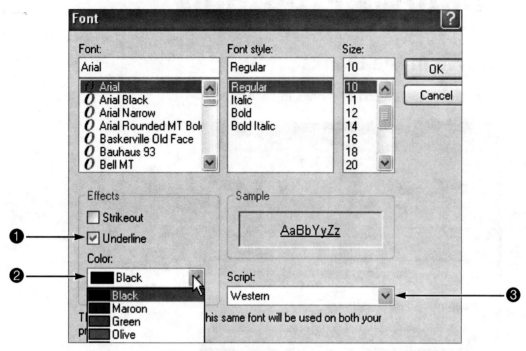

A WordPad Program Dialog Box

1. You click in the _____ to check or

uncheck them.

2. The _____

is a list of choices that opens when you click on the drop-down arrow.

3. The _____

is the arrow you click on to open the drop-down list box.

Paired Conversation

With a partner, take turns reading the A and B parts of the conversation. Fill in each blank using the vocabulasry words and computer verbs in the Word Bank.

WORD BANK

minimize	maximize	hardware	software
dialog boxes	settings	computer game	play
check	clear		

Student A	Yesterday we learned how to _____ a window.
Student B	Yes, I remember. The window disappeared but did not really close.
Student A	Do you remember how to _____ a window?
Student B	Yes. Now, let's talk about what we learned today, too.
Student A	Today we learned about _____.
Student B	Is that like the computer and the monitor?
Student A	Right. We also learned about _____.
Student B	That's like WordPad and Paint.
Student A	That's true.
Student B	We also learned about the _____.
Student A	Yes. Dialog boxes are important.
Student B	What about _____?
Student A	Settings are easy to change. They decide so many things.
Student B	Did you play a _____ today?
Student A	Not really. I just watched somebody else _____.
Student B	We did practice how to _____ boxes.
Student A	Then we learned how to uncheck to _____ the boxes.
Student B	Well, I'm so glad that we remember so much!

Vocabulary Worksheet

Fill in the blanks. Select the best answer for each sentence using the vocabulary words in the Word Bank.

WORD BANK

drop-down list arrow	checkbox	hardware
drop-down list box	dialog box	software
settings	appearance	

1. _____ is the physical part of the computer system, such as the monitor and the keyboard.

2. A _____ is a box with a list that appears from top to bottom with more things you can do.

3. A window with boxes you can check to select what you want is called a _____.

4. A _____ is a box that you can check to select something you want.

5. An arrow you can click to make the drop-down list appear is called a _____.

6. _____ are information about how a program is set up.

7. Everything in the computer system that is not hardware is called _____.

8. The way something looks is called its _____.

Verb Worksheet

Fill in the blanks. Select the best answer for each sentence using the computer verbs in the Word Bank.

WORD BANK

appear	check	clear
let up	play	preview
release	view	hold

1. You can _____ a document to see how it will look when you print it.

2. To _____ is to show on the screen so you can see it.

3. To uncheck a box is called to _____ it.

4. To _____ means to click the box so that a checkmark appears.

5. To look at something is to _____ it.

6. To _____ means to use a computer game.

7. To keep your finger pressed on the mouse button is to _____ the button.

8. To _____ means to take your finger off of the mouse button.

9. To _____ means to release or let go of a button.

Fill in the Blanks

Fill in the missing words in the sentences below. Look at the picture of the Windows Calculator to help you.

EXERCISE A: ADD TWO NUMBERS

1. Click the first _____.

2. Click the _____ sign.

3. Click the _____.

4. Click the _____ sign.

EXERCISE B: SUBTRACT TWO NUMBERS

1. Click the _____.

2. Click the _____ sign.

3. Click the _____.

4. Click the _____ sign.

EXERCISE C: MULTIPLY TWO NUMBERS

1. Click the first _____.

2. Click the _____ sign.

3. Click the _____.

4. Click the _____ sign.

Partner Activity: Practice Reading and Pronunciation

Your teacher will read the paragraphs below as you listen to the pronunciation. Then, with a partner, take turns reading the paragraphs for one minute. The listening partner will circle words that the reader needs to practice pronouncing. Alternate reading, and listening and circling words with your partner. If you get to the end of the paragraphs before the minute ends, begin reading at the beginning. Each partner should practice reading two or three times. Ask your teacher for assistance, as needed.

PRACTICE READING

Learning how to use Windows programs has been very interesting. It has also been a lot of fun. Learning the vocabulary words and verbs that explain the programs is important. It helps you understand what you read in each lesson. Let's talk a little about what you have learned.

Most programs have some type of dialog box. You can change settings by changing the information in a dialog box. Many dialog boxes have the same things, like checkboxes and drop-down list boxes. A drop-down list is a list of choices that opens when you click on it.

One of the most interesting programs that you learned how to use was the Paint program. Every Windows computer has the Paint program. You can draw pictures with the Paint program. Paint has many tools you can use to make pictures. Some tools are easy to use and some take a while to learn, but it is a lot of fun to learn how to use them all. In Paint, you can use tools on a toolbar by clicking on them. When you click on a tool, a special symbol shows for the mouse pointer. Each tool has its own symbol. You didn't use all of the tools, only a few to see how they work. You also learned that tools only work in the white area of the Paint window. If you want to pick a color, you have to click on one of the colors near the bottom of the screen. All in all, it was a very good experience to learn how to use the Paint program.

What I Have Learned

Take some time to think about what you have learned in Lesson 3. With a partner, take turns asking each other the questions in Exercise A and discussing the topics in Exercise B below.

EXERCISE A

Ask your partner the questions below. Begin each question with "Did you learn…." Your partner's answer should either be "Yes, I did" or "No, I didn't." Circle the answer that your partner provides.

"Did you learn…"		
• To open a dialog box?	Yes	No
• To make a selection from a drop-down list?	Yes	No
• To use the Paint program?	Yes	No
• To use Paint tools?	Yes	No
• To draw a box?	Yes	No
• To check a checkbox?	Yes	No
• To play a game?	Yes	No
• To use the Calculator?	Yes	No

When both you and your partner have finished asking and answering the questions, look at the "No" answers on your sheet. Study and practice your book some more. Continue asking each other these questions until both of you can answer "Yes" to all of the questions.

EXERCISE B

Talk about the topics below with your partner. Do you agree or disagree with your partner? Discuss your responses.

• Name two different types of programs.

• Name two parts of the Paint program window.

• Name two tools you find in the Paint program.

• Name two things you find in a dialog box.

• Describe how to find a game.

Crossword Puzzle

Fill in the words across and down to complete the puzzle.

ACROSS

3. A list that appears from top to bottom with more things you can choose

7. To look at something

11. When something shows and you can see it

12. To click the box so that a checkmark appears

13. Information about how a program is set up

14. A box that you can check to choose something that you want

15. The physical part of the computer system

16. To use a computer game

DOWN

1. An arrow that you can click to make the drop-down list appear

2. To keep your finger pressed on the mouse button

4. To see how information will look when it prints

5. To release or let go of the mouse button

6. Everything in the computer system that is not hardware

8. The way something looks

9. A window with boxes you can check to select what you want

10. To take your finger off the mouse button

14. To click a button or box to remove what was there before

Creating a Document in WordPad

WORKBOOK 4.1 Fill in the Computer Keyboard

On each key in this picture of the keyboard, write the letter, number, or symbol from your computer keyboard. (Your keyboard may look a little different.)

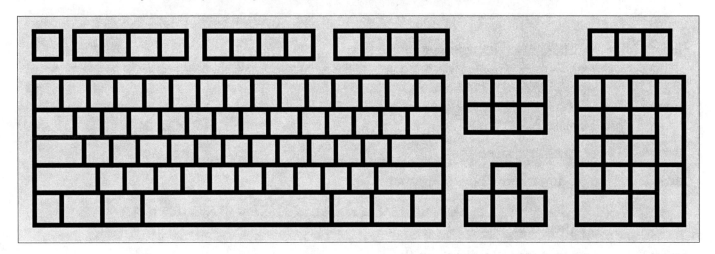

Paired Conversation

With a partner, take turns reading the A and B parts of the conversation. Fill in each blank using the vocabulary words and computer verbs in the Word Bank.

WORD BANK

computer	type	WordPad	Start button	title bar
cursor	text	Enter key	Shift key	Backspace key

Student A	Hello. Are you learning to use the _____?
Student B	Yes, I am.
Student A	Will you show me how to _____ a letter to my sister?
Student B	Yes. First, open the _____ program.
Student A	I don't know how to do that.
Student B	Click the _____. Go to All Programs, Accessories, then click WordPad.
Student A	Oh! I see "WordPad" on the _____!
Student B	Do you see the _____ blinking on the screen?
Student A	Yes, I do.
Student B	The computer is telling you that it is ready for you to type your _____.
Student A	Is there anything else that I should know before I start?
Student B	Yes. At the end of a paragraph, press the _____.
Student A	OK. Anything else?
Student B	When you want a capital letter, hold the _____ down and type the letter.
Student A	Oh. That's good to know.
Student B	You can also erase a word with the _____.
Student A	Thanks so much for helping me.
Student B	I'm sure your sister will be happy to get your letter.

Vocabulary Worksheet

Fill in the blanks. Select the best answer for each sentence using the vocabulary words in the Word Bank.

WORD BANK

cursor	Shift key	Enter key
arrow keys	Delete key	Backspace key
spacebar	text	printer

1. When you make a mistake and want to take away the letter or word you just typed, and the cursor is at the end of the word, you can use the

   _____.

2. When you want to capitalize a letter, you press the

   _____ and the letter you want to capitalize at

   the same time.

3. When you want to start a new sentence on the next line, you use the

   _____.

4. The _____ shows you where you are going to

   type text.

5. The words that you type are called _____.

6. Two ways to erase a letter or word are to use the Backspace key and to use the

   _____.

7. When you want to put a space between two words, you need to use the

   _____.

8. When you want your cursor to go to another place in the text without erasing, you can use the _____.

9. A machine that puts information on a sheet of paper from the computer is called a _____.

WORKBOOK 4.4 Verb Worksheet

Fill in the blanks. Select the best answer for each sentence using the computer verbs in the Word Bank.

WORD BANK

delete	enter	type
wrap	insert	print

1. When you want to take away a word, you need to _____ it.

2. To _____ when typing text is to go to the next line.

3. When you want to add a word between two other words, you can _____ the word.

4. To _____ means to make the words automatically continue on the next line.

5. To _____ is to use the keyboard to put information on a page.

6. To put a document from your computer onto a sheet of paper is called to _____.

Identify and Match

Complete the exercises that follow according to the directions.

EXERCISE A
Identify and name the following programs according to their icons.

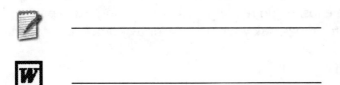

_____

_____

EXERCISE B
Match the items in Column 1 with the items in Column 2. Write the correct letter from Column 2 on the line next to the number in Column 1.

Column 1

_____ 1. WordPad

_____ 2. Word Wrap

_____ 3. Delete Key

_____ 4. Word

_____ 5. Backspace Key

_____ 6. Cursor

Column 2

A. A blinking line that shows where the computer will put the next word

B. A powerful word processor that you must buy separately and install on a computer

C. The key that deletes letters to the left ⬅ of the cursor; you remove one letter or space each time you tap it

D. A simple word processor that comes with every Windows computer

E. The key that deletes letters to the right ➡ of the cursor; you remove one letter or space each time you tap it

F. When you are typing and reach the end of a line, this feature will automatically put the following words you type on the next line for you

Partner Activity: Practice Reading and Pronunciation

Your teacher will read the paragraphs below as you listen to the pronunciation. Then, with a partner, take turns reading the paragraphs for one minute. The listening partner will circle words that the reader needs to practice pronouncing. Alternate reading, and listening and circling words with your partner. If you get to the end of the paragraphs before the minute ends, begin reading at the beginning. Each partner should practice reading two or three times. Ask your teacher for assistance, as needed.

PRACTICE READING

You use a keyboard to type on the computer. The computer keyboard has more keys than a typewriter does. Typing on a keyboard is important to learn. You should study the keyboard to learn where your fingers should be. You have to practice quite a bit to learn how to type well. Everything you type appears at the cursor position. The cursor is a blinking line that shows where the computer will type next. You can move the cursor anywhere you have typed.

Word processing programs are software programs you can use to write letters, notes, lists, and many other documents. There are two commonly used word processing programs: WordPad and Word. WordPad is a simple word processor that comes with every Windows computer. Word is a powerful word processor that you must buy separately and install on your computer. Every person has different needs and you should decide for yourself if you want a simple word processing program or if you need a more powerful word processing program.

You will often want to print documents that you type. Most programs have two methods you can use to give the print command. Both methods send what is open on your screen to the printer. When you click Print, your computer sends the document to the printer and the printer puts it onto the paper. It feels great when you print the work you have completed. You can keep it, file it, mail it, or just look at it and feel happy that you have accomplished something.

What I Have Learned

Take some time to think about what you have learned in Lesson 4. With a partner, take turns asking each other the questions in Exercise A and discussing the topics in Exercise B below.

EXERCISE A

Ask your partner the questions below. Begin each question with "Can you...."
Your partner's answer should either be "Yes, I can" or "No, I can't." Circle the answer that your partner provides.

"Can you..."		
• Place your hands on the keyboard correctly?	Yes	No
• Use the keyboard to type something?	Yes	No
• Identify the cursor when you see it?	Yes	No
• Insert a title in a document?	Yes	No
• Delete text from a document?	Yes	No
• Identify and use the Backspace key?	Yes	No
• Send your work to the printer?	Yes	No
• Type a list?	Yes	No

When both you and your partner have finished asking and answering the questions, look at the "No" answers on your sheet. Study and practice your book some more. Continue asking each other these questions until both of you can answer "Yes" to all of the questions.

EXERCISE B

Talk about the topics below with your partner. Do you agree or disagree with your partner? Discuss your responses.

• Name two common keys on a computer keyboard.

• Explain what word wrap is.

• Tell me where the cursor appears.

• Explain what the spacebar is used for.

• Explain what are the arrow keys are used for.

Crossword Puzzle

Fill in the words across and down to complete the puzzle.

ACROSS

2. To use the keyboard to type information on the page

4. To type text between two other pieces of text

7. Push it down when you want a capital letter or the top symbol on the key

9. To put a document from your computer onto a sheet of paper

12. To take away or erase

14. Shows where you are going to type text

15. Place the cursor after the letter or word and push this key to erase

DOWN

1. Use this to go to the next line when you finish putting information on a line

3. A machine that puts information from the computer onto a sheet of paper

5. Use this when you want to start text on another line

6. Words and letters that you write or type on paper

8. Puts an empty space between your words

10. Use these to move your cursor to another place without erasing

11. Place the cursor in front of a letter and push this key to erase

13. To make the words automatically go to the next line

Doing More with WordPad

WORKBOOK 5.1 Fill in the Blanks

Write the correct word that goes in each blank.

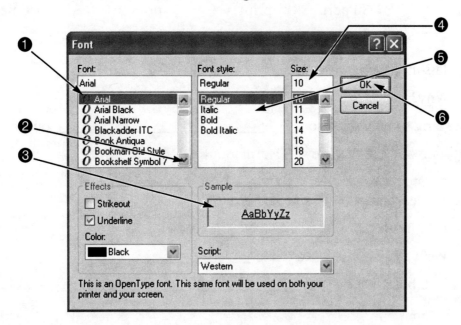

1. In the _____ _____,

   you choose the font name to change the font type.

2. You click on the _____

   _____ to see more font types.

3. The _____ _____

   shows what the text will look like.

4. In the _____ _____,

   you choose a number to change text to a different size.

5. You choose regular, bold, or italic in the _____

   _____ _____.

6. When you are finished, click the _____

   _____.

Paired Conversation

With a partner, take turns reading the A and B parts of the conversation. Fill in each blank using the vocabulary words and computer verbs in the Word Bank.

WORD BANK

format	fonts	bold	italic	USB drive
insert	USB port	print	printer	document

Student A	Today's lesson is going to be fun.
Student B	Really? Why?
Student A	We are going to learn how to _____ our text.
Student B	I heard someone say that we will learn about _____.
Student A	Yes, we will learn how to change our text.
Student B	That sounds like fun!
Student A	I know. We'll also learn how to make _____ text.
Student B	That's good, but I like the way _____ text looks better.
Student A	Well, we will learn both!
Student B	Did you bring your _____?
Student A	Yes, I did, but I don't know how to _____ it in the computer.
Student B	I'll show you how to put it in the _____.
Student A	Thanks. I don't want to mess it up.
Student B	We can put all this new stuff in our own documents.
Student A	Do you think we will be able to _____ today?
Student B	I think so.
Student A	We have a nice _____ in the classroom.
Student B	Well, I'm going to be the first one to print my _____!

Vocabulary Worksheet

Fill in the blanks. Select the best answer for each sentence using the vocabulary words in the Word Bank.

WORD BANK

document	alignment	USB drive
USB port	font	bullets
bold	italic	

1. The _____ is the design and size of the letters.

2. A style of lettering where the letters are thicker and darker is called _____.

3. _____ are special characters that you can put before items on a list.

4. Something written that provides information is called a _____.

5. _____ is when information is placed on one side or in the center.

6. A _____ is a small opening on the CPU where you insert the USB drive.

7. A style of lettering where the letters are a little slanted to the right is called _____.

8. A small tool that is used to save computer files and that you can use in different computers is called a _____.

Fill in the blanks. Select the best answer for each sentence using the computer verbs in the Word Bank.

WORD BANK

save	decrease	highlight
insert	align	format
increase	scroll	right-click

1. To bring text into line on one side or in the center is to

   _____ text.

2. To _____ means to keep what you did on a

   document in the computer so you can use it again later.

3. To pick the font that you want and to use it in your document is to

   _____ .

4. To _____ means to put a USB drive into the USB

   port of a computer.

5. To make your text smaller in size is to _____ it.

6. To _____ text, you click at the beginning of a

   letter and drag the mouse to the end of what you want to change.

7. To press and release the right mouse button is to

   _____ .

8. To _____ means to move the contents of a

   window up, down, right, or left.

9. To _____ the text means to make the text bigger

   in size.

Fill in the Blanks

Complete Exercise A, Exercise B, and Exercise C as instructed below.

EXERCISE A
Identify the types of font formatting used in the following examples.

Example	Font Format
1. ABC	_____
2. **ABC**	_____
3. *ABC*	_____
4. <u>ABC</u>	_____

EXERCISE B
Identify the alignment buttons shown below.

Example	Alignment Type
1.	_____
2.	_____
3.	_____

EXERCISE C
Fill in the blanks to complete each sentence about how to highlight text.

1. Click at the _____ end of the text that you want to highlight.

2. Continue to hold down the left _____ as you move to the left and up (drag).

3. Let go of the mouse button when all of the _____ is selected.

Partner Activity: Practice Reading and Pronunciation

Your teacher will read the paragraphs below as you listen to the pronunciation. Then, with a partner, take turns reading the paragraphs for one minute. The listening partner will circle words that the reader needs to practice pronouncing. Alternate reading, and listening and circling words with your partner. If you get to the end of the paragraphs before the minute ends, begin reading at the beginning. Each partner should practice reading two or three times. Ask your teacher for assistance, as needed.

PRACTICE READING

Learning to do more things with WordPad is very interesting. Changing text is really an exciting learning process. To change the format of text, you must highlight it first. You can see that text is highlighted when the background becomes black. People like to format text to make the text look better and more appealing. One way you can make text look different is by changing the font style. There are many different font styles. You can have fun looking at all of the different font styles to see which one you want to use. There are other ways to format text. For example, you can make your text bold, italic, or even underlined.

You can add bullets to whatever you type to make lines of text look more like a list. If you want to add bullets, you have to highlight the lines where you want the bullets. Then, click the Bullets button on the toolbar. When you finish, you will see that you have bullets.

What I Have Learned

Take some time to think about what you have learned in Lesson 5. With a partner, take turns asking each other the questions in Exercise A and discussing the topics in Exercise B below.

EXERCISE A

Ask your partner the questions below. Begin each question with "Did you learn...." Your partner's answer should either be "Yes, I did" or "No, I didn't." Circle the answer that your partner provides.

"Did you learn..."		
• To highlight text?	Yes	No
• To change the font style?	Yes	No
• To add bullets?	Yes	No
• To change alignment?	Yes	No
• To name a file?	Yes	No
• To save a file?	Yes	No
• How to insert a USB drive into a USB port?	Yes	No
• How to remove a USB drive?	Yes	No
• To create a list?	Yes	No

When both you and your partner have finished asking and answering the questions, look at the "No" answers on your sheet. Study and practice your book some more. Continue asking each other these questions until both of you can answer "Yes" to all of the questions.

EXERCISE B

Talk about the topics below with your partner. Do you agree or disagree with your partner? Discuss your responses.

• Tell me how to insert a USB drive into the computer.

• Explain when you need to highlight text.

• Tell me how to tell if text is highlighted.

• Describe what right-click means.

• Describe how to make a regular text sentence in bold text.

Crossword Puzzle

Fill in the words across and down to complete the puzzle.

ACROSS

1. A small tool used to save computer files

5. To move around in a window

8. A machine that puts information from the computer onto a sheet of paper

11. A style of lettering where the letters are slanted to the right

13. To put a USB drive into the USB port of a computer

14. To keep what you did on the computer so you can use it at a later time

15. To make something smaller

DOWN

2. Something that is written and provides information

3. A style of lettering where the letters are wider and darker

4. A small opening on the CPU where you insert a USB drive

6. To press and release the right mouse button

7. When information is placed on one side or in the center

9. Special character that you can put before items in a list

10. The kind of lettering used in text to make it look a certain way

11. To make something bigger

12. To bring into line on one side or in the center

Using the Internet

WORKBOOK 6.1 Fill in the Blanks

Write the correct word that goes in each blank.

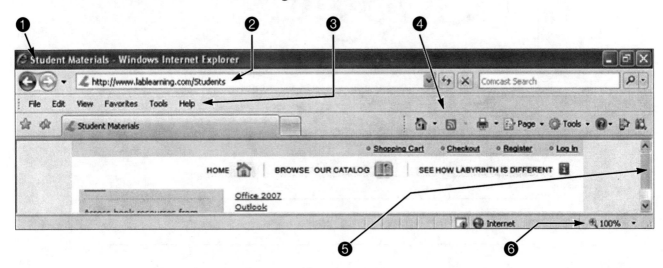

1. The _____ tells you the website you are visiting and that you are using Internet Explorer.

2. On the _____, you can see the address (or URL) of the website you are visiting. You can also click here and type the address of the website you want to go to.

3. Internet Explorer has a special _____ for using the Internet.

4. Internet Explorer has a special _____ for using the Internet.

5. The _____ lets you move to parts of the website that you cannot see yet.

6. The _____ shows you where you are on the Internet and your progress to where you are going.

WORKBOOK 6.2 **Fill in the Blanks**

Write the correct word that goes in each blank.

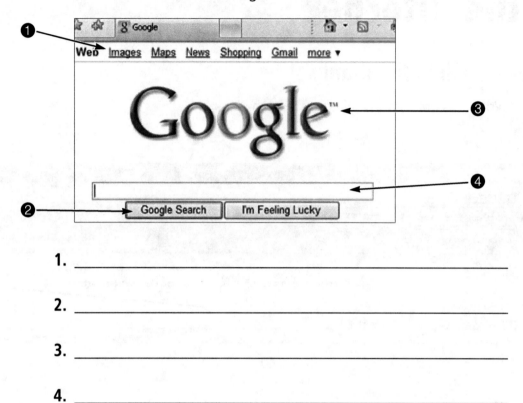

1. _____

2. _____

3. _____

4. _____

Paired Conversation

With a partner, take turns reading the A and B parts of the conversation. Fill in each blank using the vocabulary words and computer verbs in the Word Bank.

WORD BANK

student	classroom	Internet	websites	search engine
Internet	visit	go	homepage	connect
URL	hyperlinks	browse	simulation	search

Student A	I'm a new _____.
Student B	Welcome to our _____!
Student A	I heard that today's class is about the _____.
Student B	That's right.
Student A	Which _____ will we visit?
Student B	I'm not sure. We'll have to use a _____.
Student A	Is that what you use to look for things on the _____?
Student B	That's right.
Student A	Well, let's _____ an interesting website.
Student B	I know! Let's _____ to our school's _____ first.
Student A	That's a great idea. Let's _____ to it now.
Student B	Well, let's type in the _____ for our school.
Student A	OK. Now what do I do?
Student B	We can use the _____ to go to the pages we want.
Student A	Thanks. Now I want to _____ the Internet.
Student B	You'll have to wait. We have to do a _____ exercise first.
Student A	OK.
Student B	Later, we can _____ for other interesting subjects.

Vocabulary Worksheet

Fill in the blanks. Select the best answer for each sentence using the vocabulary words in the Word Bank.

WORD BANK

Internet	modem	hyperlink	Internet connection
scroll bar	website	URL	web browser
simulation	ISP	homepage	search engine

1. An object or text that takes you from one web page to another when you click on it is called a _____.

2. A company that provides a connection to the Internet, usually for a fee, is called an _____.

3. The _____ is a system of computers from all over the world that are connected so they can communicate.

4. The page that opens when you open Internet Explorer is called the

   _____.

5. A _____ is a tool that connects your computer to the Internet.

6. Software that lets you connect to the Internet is called a

   _____.

7. A _____ is an exercise that is not real. It is planned ahead of time, with all of the possibilities already set.

8. A place on the Internet where you can find information by using a search engine or an address is called a _____.

9. An _____ is the system that connects you to the Internet.

10. A website you can use to look for things on the Internet is called a _____.

11. A _____ lets you move to parts of a website that you cannot yet see.

12. The unique address for each web page is called a _____.

Verb Worksheet

Fill in the blanks. Select the best answer for each sentence using the computer verbs in the Word Bank. You can use some of the words twice.

WORD BANK

browse	connect
search	visit

1. To look at an Internet website is to _____ it.

2. When you _____ to the Internet, you make contact with it.

3. To _____ the Internet means to look around on different websites.

4. To look for information on a specific topic on the Internet is called to _____ .

5. I have half an hour to _____ the Internet and see if I can find a gift for my brother's birthday.

6. I am writing a book report. I will _____ the Internet for facts about my topic.

Identify and Match

Match the items in Column 1 with the items in Column 2. Write the correct letter from Column 2 on the line next to the number in Column 1. (Hint: There are five different types of Internet connections included.)

Column 1

_____ **1.** Dial-up

_____ **2.** Internet

_____ **3.** Scroll bars

_____ **4.** Cable

_____ **5.** Wi-Fi

_____ **6.** Homepage

_____ **7.** Satellite

_____ **8.** Search engine

_____ **9.** DSL

Column 2

A. Internet connection that uses the same cable that cable television uses

B. The first page Internet Explorer shows when you start the program

C. A website made to look for things on the Internet (for example, Google.com, Yahoo.com, and Ask.com)

D. Internet connection that uses a regular telephone line to connect to the Internet; the slowest type of connection

E. You must have a special telephone line to use this type of Internet connection

F. Wireless networking sends the Internet data through the air; no wires or cables are needed

G. Millions of computers from all parts of the world connected so they can communicate

H. These are used to move around in a window

I. A cable connects you to a satellite dish, which communicates with a satellite for Internet access

Partner Activity: Practice Reading and Pronunciation

Your teacher will read the paragraphs below as you listen to the pronunciation. Then, with a partner, take turns reading the paragraphs for one minute. The listening partner will circle words that the reader needs to practice pronouncing. Alternate reading, and listening and circling words with your partner. If you get to the end of the paragraphs before the minute ends, begin reading at the beginning. Each partner should practice reading two or three times. Ask your teacher for assistance, as needed.

PRACTICE READING

The Internet is millions of computers from all parts of the world connected so they can communicate. To join the Internet, you must have an Internet connection. You get one by signing up with an Internet service provider. There are a few different ways to connect to the Internet. For each type of connection, you should be able to find multiple providers in your area.

You need special software on your computer to connect to the Internet. That special software is called an Internet browser. Many people use Internet Explorer as their browser.

A search engine is a website made to look for things on the Internet. Google is one of the many search engines you can use. Search engines change very often, and each one looks different. For example, Google.com looks different from Yahoo.com, which looks different from Ask.com.

When you get results from a search engine, take a few minutes to look at them. You have to decide which one gives you what you want. Sometimes you have to go to a few search engines to find what you want.

What I Have Learned

Take some time to think about what you have learned in Lesson 6. With a partner, take turns asking each other the questions in Exercise A and discussing the topics in Exercise B below.

EXERCISE A

Ask your partner the questions below. Begin each question with "Can you…." Your partner's answer should either be "Yes, I can" or "No, I can't." Circle the answer that your partner provides.

"Can you…"		
• Open Internet Explorer?	Yes	No
• Type an address in the address bar?	Yes	No
• Use a search engine to find information?	Yes	No
• Type a URL to go to a website?	Yes	No
• Use vocabulary words to describe using Internet Explorer?	Yes	No
• Use scroll bars to move around a window?	Yes	No
• Read a web page?	Yes	No
• Fill out a form online?	Yes	No

When both you and your partner have finished asking and answering the questions, look at the "No" answers on your sheet. Study and practice your book some more. Continue asking each other these questions until both of you can answer "Yes" to all the questions.

EXERCISE B

Talk about the topics below with your partner. Do you agree or disagree with your partner? Discuss your responses.

• Name three different search engines.

• Explain how to go to a website.

• Tell me where to find the scroll bars.

• Describe a search engine.

• Tell me how to search for a state governor.

Crossword Puzzle

Fill in the words across and down to complete the puzzle.

ACROSS

3. The page that appears when you open Internet Explorer

6. Software that lets you connect to the Internet

7. A company that gives you a connection to the Internet

8. The unique address for each Web page

10. To look around on the Internet

14. The system that lets you make contact with the Internet

15. To look at an Internet Web site

16. To look for information on a specific topic on the Internet

DOWN

1. A piece of equipment that connects your computer to the Internet

2. The place on the Internet where you can find information

4. A website you can use to look for things on the Internet

5. An exercise that is planned ahead of time, with all the possibilities already set

9. To make contact with the Internet

11. An object or text that takes you from one web page to another when you click on it

12. The device that lets you move to other parts of a website

13. Computers from all over the world connected so they can communicate

Working with Email

WORKBOOK 7.1 Fill in the Blanks

Write the correct word or words in each blank.

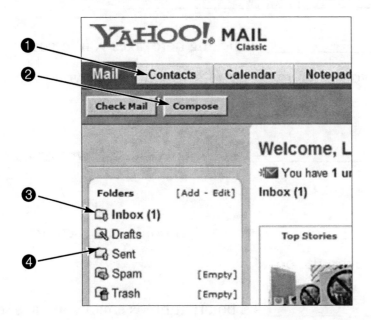

1. _____

2. _____

3. _____

4. _____

Fill in the Blanks

Write the correct word that goes in each blank.

WORD BANK

Inbox	Compose
Contacts	Sent

1. _____ – Clicking here takes you to your

   Contacts list, where you enter and keep addresses of people you want

   to email.

2. _____ – You click here to start writing a new

   message.

3. _____ – A box that holds email sent to you.

   You click this link to open the box.

4. _____ – A box that holds email you have sent.

   You click this link to open the box.

Fill in the Blanks

Write the correct words from the Word Bank that go in each blank.

WORD BANK

The email message	Click if you want to answer the message	Email address of person who sent the message
Click to send the message to someone else	Date and time message was sent	Click to delete the message

1. _____

2. _____

3. _____

4. _____

5. _____

6. _____

With a partner, take turns reading the A and B parts of the conversation. Fill in each blank using the vocabulary words and computers verbs in the Word Bank.

WORD BANK

message	email	send	reply	compose
webmail	username	password	Inbox	

Student A	Hi. What are you doing?
Student B	I'm writing a _____ to my friend in India.
Student A	Really? How will you send it?
Student B	I'll send it to him by _____.
Student A	Is it easy to _____ an email all the way to India?
Student B	Sure it is. It's easy to _____, too.
Student A	I want to _____ and send a message, but I don't have email.
Student B	Well, you can get a _____ account.
Student A	How much does it cost?
Student B	Sometimes webmail is free.
Student A	Really? Will you help me?
Student B	Sure. You need to choose the name you want to use.
Student A	Is that what a _____ is? Do I also need a _____?
Student B	Yes, you do.
Student A	OK. Now please tell me what an Inbox is.
Student B	My _____ is on the screen now. It shows me a list of the email messages that I received.

Vocabulary Worksheet

Fill in the blanks. Select the best answer for each sentence using the vocabulary words in the Word Bank.

WORD BANK

message	button	email	password
Inbox	username	webmail	"at" symbol

1. The character that is included in email addresses between the username and the provider name is called the _____.

2. _____ means electronic mail. It is a way to send information from one computer to another.

3. The name that you choose for your personal email account is called your _____.

4. A _____ is a personal word or combination of letters and numbers that allows you access to your email.

5. Information that you type and send to another person using email is called a _____.

6. _____ is an email service that allows you to reach your email account from computers other than your own.

7. A page in your email that lists all of the messages you have received is the _____.

8. A small rectangle that completes an action when you click it is called a _____.

Verb Worksheet

Fill in the blanks. Select the best answer for each sentence using the computer verbs in the Word Bank. You may use the words more than once.

WORD BANK

compose	send	forward	reply

1. To receive a message and then send it on to another person is to

   _____ the message.

2. To _____ a message means to pass it from your

   email to another person's email.

3. To _____ a message means to write a message.

4. To answer a message that you received is to

   _____ to it.

5. I want to let my piano teacher know how much she has helped me, so I

   will _____ a nice message to show my

   appreciation and send it to her.

6. I received a message from my cousin asking about our airline tickets to

   Hawaii. I need to _____ and let her know that I

   already bought the tickets.

7. Tomorrow is Mary's birthday. I will _____ her a

   message and wish her a happy birthday.

8. I got a very funny email message today. Do you want me to

   _____ it to you so you can read it?

Identify and Match

Match the items in Column 1 with the items in Column 2. Write the correct letter from Column 2 on the line next to the number in Column 1.

Column 1

_____ 1. Internet access

_____ 2. Email message

_____ 3. Webmail

_____ 4. Contacts

_____ 5. Email

_____ 6. Yahoo!

_____ 7. Password

_____ 8. student@msn.com

Column 2

A. Using this is a fast and easy way to communicate to all people in the world who have Internet access.

B. This company's webmail is one of the most used.

C. This is a sample email address.

D. You must have an email address and this to use email.

E. When you get an email account, you must pick a username and this to access your account.

F. Sending one of these is like sending a letter through the mail.

G. This is useful because you can use it from any computer in the world that has Internet access. Many companies offer it for free.

H. This is a list of names and email addresses in an email address book.

Partner Activity: Practice Reading and Pronunciation

Your teacher will read the paragraphs below as you listen to the pronunciation. Then, with a partner, take turns reading the paragraphs for one minute. The listening partner will circle words that the reader needs to practice pronouncing. Alternate reading, and listening and circling words with your partner. If you get to the end of the paragraphs before the minute ends, begin reading at the beginning. Each partner should practice reading two or three times. Ask your teacher for assistance, as needed.

PRACTICE READING

Using email is a fast and easy way to communicate to people all over the world who have Internet access. You must have an email address and Internet access to use email. All Internet service providers give you an email address when you sign up with them. When you get an email account, you can send and receive email. Email has become one of the most common ways to communicate all over the world. You can send emails to your friends and family members even when you are far away from home, in another country, or even on another continent.

An email address must have three parts: a username, the "at" symbol, and an email service provider name. The email address cannot have spaces. When you get an email account, you must pick a username and a password. The name is the special name that you use to access your email. A password is important because it keeps your email safe. No one can read your email unless they have your username and password. You should keep your password secret and safe at all times.

Sending an email message is like sending a written letter. You must add the email address of the person who will get the email. With email, you can also take an email that you have received and send it to somebody else. This is called forwarding an email, and it is a very popular and useful feature. With email, you can reach more people easier and much faster than you can with written letters.

What I Have Learned

Take some time to think about what you have learned in Lesson 7. With a partner, take turns asking each other the questions in Exercise A and discussing the topics in Exercise B below.

EXERCISE A

Ask your partner the questions below. Begin each question with "Did you learn…." Your partner's answer should either be "Yes, I did" or "No, I didn't." Circle the answer that your partner provides.

"Did you learn…"		
• To sign up for webmail?	Yes	No
• To sign in to email?	Yes	No
• To use the Compose button?	Yes	No
• To type an email address?	Yes	No
• To check for new email?	Yes	No
• To type an email message?	Yes	No
• To send an email message?	Yes	No
• To reply to an email message?	Yes	No
• To forward an email message?	Yes	No
• To delete an email message?	Yes	No

When both you and your partner have finished asking and answering the questions, look at the "No" answers on your sheet. Study and practice your book some more. Continue asking each other these questions until both of you can answer "Yes" to all the questions.

EXERCISE B

Talk about the topics below with your partner. Do you agree or disagree with your partner? Discuss your responses.

• Tell me how to sign up for webmail.

• Explain why you think email is important.

• Tell me how to get an email address.

• Tell me where to keep my email addresses.

Crossword Puzzle

Fill in the words across and down to complete the puzzle.

ACROSS

1. The character that is included in email addresses between the username and the provider name

6. The name you choose for your personal email account

8. A page in your email that lists all the messages you have received

9. To transmit a message from your email to another person's email

10. To write a message

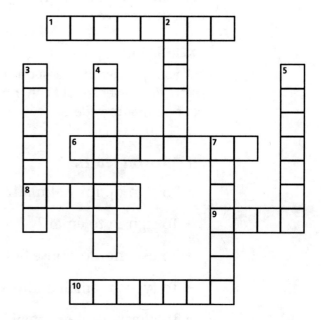

DOWN

2. A small rectangle that completes an action when you click it

3. An email service that allows you to reach your email account from computers other than your own

4. A personal word or combination of letters and numbers that allows you access to your email

5. To send a message that you received on to another person

7. Information that you type and send to another person using email

Writing Letters in Microsoft Word

WORKBOOK 8.1 Fill in the Blanks

Write the correct word that goes in each blank.

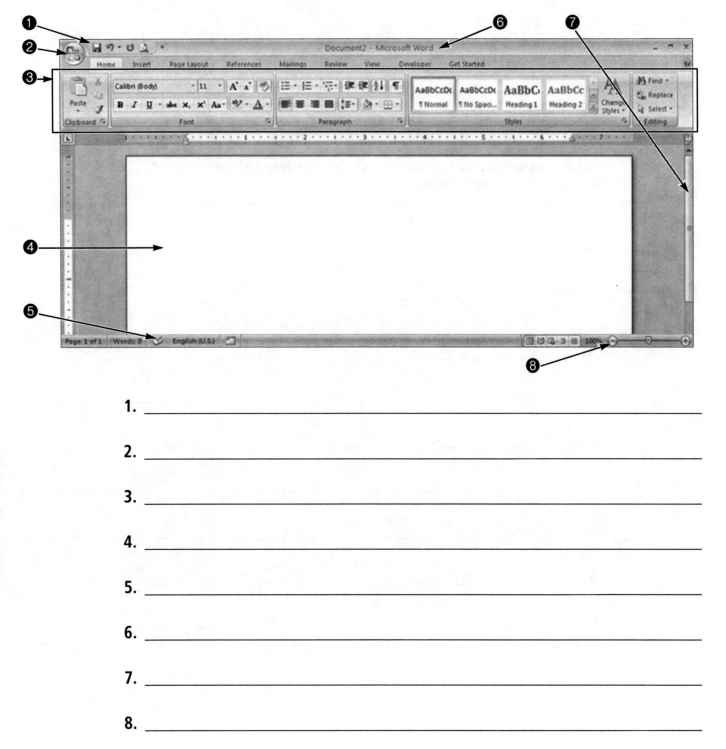

1. _____

2. _____

3. _____

4. _____

5. _____

6. _____

7. _____

8. _____

Fill in the Blanks

Write the correct word in each blank.

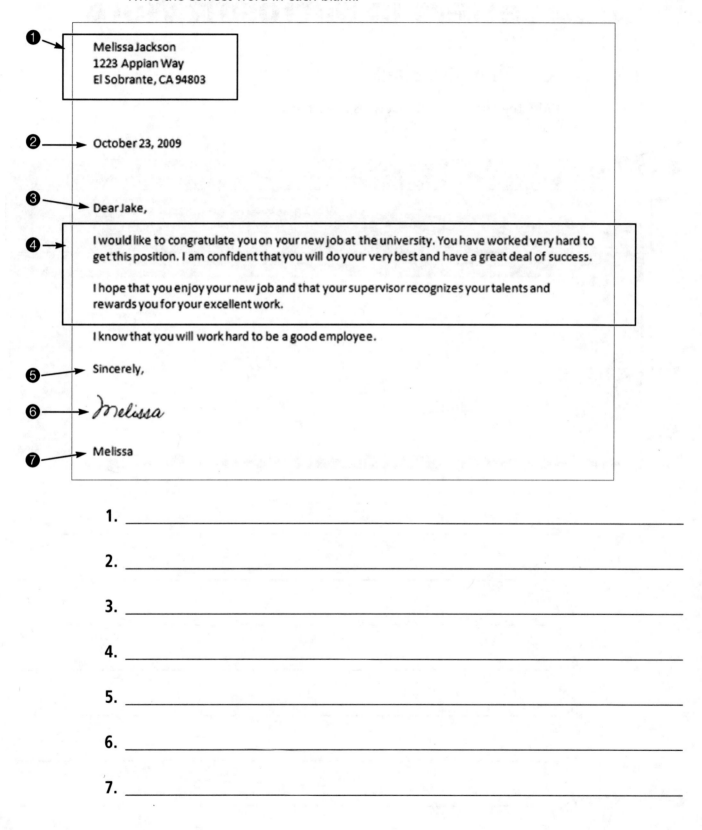

Melissa Jackson
1223 Appian Way
El Sobrante, CA 94803

October 23, 2009

Dear Jake,

I would like to congratulate you on your new job at the university. You have worked very hard to get this position. I am confident that you will do your very best and have a great deal of success.

I hope that you enjoy your new job and that your supervisor recognizes your talents and rewards you for your excellent work.

I know that you will work hard to be a good employee.

Sincerely,

Melissa

Melissa

1. _____

2. _____

3. _____

4. _____

5. _____

6. _____

7. _____

Paired Conversation

With a partner, take turns reading the A and B parts of the conversation. Fill in each blank using the vocabulary words and computer verbs in the Word Bank.

WORD BANK

composing	greeting	business letter	format	font
Word Ribbon	buttons	ScreenTips	closing	spelling

Student A	Hi! What's the matter?
Student B	I'm having trouble _____ a letter to my grandma.
Student A	Why are you having trouble?
Student B	Well, I can't think of a good _____.
Student A	How about "My Dearest Grandma"?
Student B	That sounds good!
Student A	Well, you don't want it to sound like a _____!
Student B	That's true!
Student A	You should _____ your letter so it will look nice.
Student B	I know. I want a nice _____.
Student A	You will need to use the _____.
Student B	I only know a little bit about the Ribbon with all the groups of _____.
Student A	You should also read the _____ when they appear.
Student B	Yes, they help me a lot.
Student A	Have you thought about a _____?
Student B	I think I will write "Your Loving Granddaughter."
Student A	That sounds great. Don't forget to check your _____!
Student B	I won't!

Fill in the blanks. Select the best answer for each sentence, using vocabulary words from the Word Bank.

WORD BANK

Word Ribbon	tab	Spelling and Grammar button	ScreenTip
greeting	salutation	closing	complimentary close
Office button	group	Quick Access toolbar	

1. The opening words of a personal letter are called the

   _____.

2. The last words before you sign a business letter are called the

   _____.

3. The _____ is the round, multicolored button at the top-left corner of the Word window.

4. A _____ is a box with information about a button that appears when you put your mouse (without clicking) over the button.

5. A special tool that checks your spelling and grammar in a typed document is called the _____.

6. The last words before you sign a personal letter are called the

   _____.

7. The _____ refers to the opening words of a business letter.

8. The _____ is composed of tabs and buttons grouped together.

9. A set of several buttons that are together in a section under a tab is called a

_____.

10. The _____ is the bar above the Word Ribbon and

to the right of the Office button. It has buttons that you use often.

11. A _____ is a small rectangle on the Word Ribbon

that you click to see different groups of buttons.

Verb Worksheet

Fill in the blanks. Select the best answer for each sentence using the computer verbs in the Word Bank.

WORD BANK

open	format	ignore
insert	check spelling	

1. To _____ means to pay no attention to something.

2. To _____ means to make design choices about the way your document looks.

3. When you _____, you review a document for spelling and grammar mistakes.

4. To put letters or words in text that is already written is to _____ the letters or words.

5. When you _____ a document, you put a saved document on the screen.

Partner Activity: Practice Reading and Pronunciation

Your teacher will read the paragraphs below as you listen to the pronunciation. Then, with a partner, take turns reading the paragraphs for one minute. The listening partner will circle words that the reader needs to practice pronouncing. Alternate reading, and listening and circling words with your partner. If you get to the end of the paragraphs before the minute ends, begin reading at the beginning. Each partner should practice reading two or three times. Ask your teacher for assistance, as needed.

PRACTICE READING

Microsoft Word is the most frequently used word processing program in the world. It does much more than WordPad. It takes awhile to learn to work with this program. But, it is really worth the time that you spend learning it. With this program, you are able to write different types of letters. You learned how to write two different types of letters in this lesson. You learned to write a personal letter and a business letter. You can write a personal letter to a friend or a relative. You can write a business letter to a professional person.

Something that is very useful in the Microsoft Word program is the Quick Access toolbar. This is a special toolbar at the top of the window. You can always see it, and it is easy to use. You can put the buttons that you use often on the Quick Access toolbar. You can add or remove buttons from this toolbar too. My Quick Access toolbar may have different buttons from yours, depending on which buttons each of us decides to include.

Another advantage that you have with this program is the ScreenTips. They are little words that appear when you place your mouse over the buttons. Every button has its own ScreenTip that describes what will happen when you click on the button.

What I Have Learned

Take some time to think about what you have learned in Lesson 8. With a partner, take turns asking each other the questions in Exercise A and discussing the topics in Exercise B below.

EXERCISE A

Ask your partner the questions below. Begin each question with "Can you…." Your partner's answer should either be "Yes, I can" or "No, I can't." Circle the answer that your partner provides.

"Can you…"		
• Open Microsoft Word?	Yes	No
• Type a personal letter?	Yes	No
• Type a business letter?	Yes	No
• Check your spelling?	Yes	No
• Start a new document?	Yes	No
• Print a file?	Yes	No
• Make changes to a letter?	Yes	No
• Use the Undo button?	Yes	No

When both you and your partner have finished asking and answering the questions, look at the "No" answers on your sheet. Study and practice your book some more. Continue asking each other these questions until both of you can answer "Yes" to all the questions.

EXERCISE B

Talk about the topics below with your partner. Do you agree or disagree with your partner? Discuss your responses.

• Name two different types of letters you can type.

• Describe how to open a saved file.

• Tell me how to find the Print Preview button.

• Name two buttons in the Clipboard group.

• Tell me how to view a ScreenTip.

• Describe what you like about the Quick Access toolbar.

Crossword Puzzle

Fill in the words down and across to complete the puzzle.

ACROSS

3. The bar above the Word Ribbon and to the right of the Office button; includes buttons you use most often

5. To pay no attention to something

7. To put a saved document on the screen

8. The last words before you sign a personal letter

9. Composed of tabs and buttons grouped together near the top of the Word window

10. The opening words for a personal letter

12. The opening words for a business letter

14. A set of several buttons that are together in a section under a tab

15. The last words before you sign a business letter

DOWN

1. A little box that appears when you put your mouse (without clicking) on a button

2. A small rectangle on the Word Ribbon that you click to see different groups of buttons

4. A special button that you click to check your spelling and grammar in a document

6. The round, multicolored button at the top-left corner of the Word window

11. To make design changes to the way your document looks

13. To put into something

Copying and Pasting

WORKBOOK 9.1 Fill in the Blanks

Write the correct word that goes in each blank.

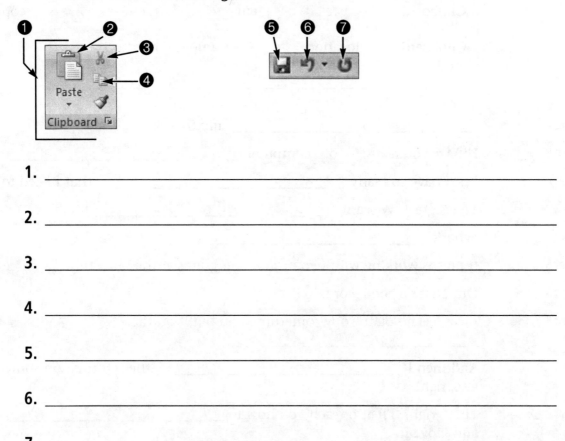

1. _____

2. _____

3. _____

4. _____

5. _____

6. _____

7. _____

Paired Conversation

With a partner, take turns reading the A and B parts of the conversation. Fill in each blank using the vocabulary words and computer verbs in the Word Bank.

WORD BANK

Greetings	lesson	files	multitask	multitasking
Clipboard	paste	cut	move	copy
Clipboard group	location	File Name box	results	

Student A	_____, my friend!
Student B	Hi! Are you ready for our computer _____ today?
Student A	Yes. I have so many _____ that I need to work on.
Student B	That's great. We can _____ today.
Student A	What's _____?
Student B	It means working with two or more programs at the same time.
Student A	Oh. That's a good word.
Student B	I will teach you to copy something and put it on the _____.
Student A	And then I _____ the information somewhere else, right?
Student B	That's right. I'll also teach you how to _____ text and move it.
Student A	I really need to learn how to cut and _____ text!
Student B	Cut, _____, and paste are all on the Clipboard group.
Student A	Is the _____ on the Word Ribbon?
Student B	Right! You seem to understand this stuff.
Student A	Thanks. I know the _____ of the files I want to work on.
Student B	Good. When you finish, type the new filename in the _____.
Student A	And I'll remember where I save it.
Student B	You're doing great. The _____ will be wonderful!

Vocabulary Worksheet

Fill in the blanks. Select the best answer for each sentence using the vocabulary words in the Word Bank.

WORD BANK

Save In box	File Name box	file	Clipboard
Clipboard group	location	result	

1. The box that appears when you want to save a document and that lets you type the name of your document is called the

   _____.

2. A _____ is the place where something is.

3. A _____ is a piece of work (such as a letter or a picture) that is saved in the computer.

4. When you copy something, it goes on the _____ before you paste it to a new location.

5. The _____ is the effect of a change you make.

6. The part of the Home tab of the Word Ribbon that holds the Copy and Paste buttons is called the _____.

7. When you want to save a document, you will see the

   _____ appear to let you choose where to save your document.

Verb Worksheet

Fill in the blanks. Select the best answer for each sentence, using the computer verbs from the Word Bank.

WORD BANK

cut	copy	paste
move	undo	multitask

1. To _____ means to change the location of text or other information.

2. To do more than one task at the same time is to _____.

3. When you _____, you take away or delete text or information you do not want.

4. To cancel the last thing that you did is called to _____.

5. To _____ means to duplicate text in a document so you can put it in a different location.

6. To _____ means to take text that you copied and to put it in a different place.

Fill in the Blanks

Fill in the blanks. Select the best answer for each blank using the vocabulary words in the Word Bank. The paragraph describes how to copy and paste.

WORD BANK

highlight	Copy	Paste	click
Clipboard	save	location	Word Ribbon

To copy information, you must _____ it first. To copy, click the _____ button on the Home tab of the _____. You will not see anything happen yet. The information you copied is now in a place on the computer called the _____. Now, _____ where you want the information to go. Then, click the _____ button on the Home tab of the Word Ribbon to put the information into your document. If you see any other buttons appear automatically, do not click them. They will go away as you do more work or after you _____ the file. The pasted information stays where it was, and it also goes to the new _____.

Partner Activity: Practice Reading and Pronunciation

Your teacher will read the paragraphs below as you listen to the pronunciation. Then, with a partner, take turns reading the paragraphs for one minute. The listening partner will circle words that the reader needs to practice pronouncing. Alternate reading, and listening and circling words with your partner. If you get to the end of the paragraphs before the minute ends, begin reading at the beginning. Each partner should practice reading two or three times. Ask your teacher for assistance, as needed.

PRACTICE READING

The lesson that you just studied taught you about some very interesting and helpful features. Sometimes you may want to repeat a word or sentence in a document. To save time, you can copy that information instead of typing it again. When you copy something, it goes to a place in the computer's memory that you cannot see. This place is called the Clipboard. The computer keeps the information there until you copy something else or close the program.

Sometimes you may want to make changes to a file but still keep the old, unchanged file. You can keep the old file under the old name and save the new file with a new name.

Undo is another very helpful feature. You use Undo to cancel the last thing you did. If you just deleted a word and you need to bring it back, you want to undo the delete. You just have to push the Undo button to make the deleted item return to the document.

The easiest way to move text is to highlight it and drag it to a new place. This is different from copying and pasting because the text does not stay where it was before. It is only in the new place. You have more choices with the documents you make if you can copy information from one program and paste it into another. You can copy pictures or text. There are so many different things to learn to make your computer experience easier and more fun.

What I Have Learned

Take some time to think about what you have learned in Lesson 9. With a partner, take turns asking each other the questions in Exercise A and discussing the topics in Exercise B below.

EXERCISE A

Ask your partner the questions below. Begin each question with "Did you learn…." Your partner's answer should either be "Yes, I did" or "No, I didn't." Circle the answer that your partner provides.

"Did you learn..."		
• To work with the Clipboard?	Yes	No
• To copy and paste text?	Yes	No
• To cut text?	Yes	No
• To save a file with a new name?	Yes	No
• To copy a picture?	Yes	No
• To use right-click to copy and paste?	Yes	No
• To work with the Word Ribbon?	Yes	No
• To use the Save In box?	Yes	No
• To undo an action?	Yes	No
• To move text from one location to another?	Yes	No

When both you and your partner have finished asking and answering the questions, look at the "No" answers on your sheet. Study and practice your book some more. Continue asking each other these questions until both of you can answer "Yes" to all the questions.

EXERCISE B

Talk about the topics below with your partner. Do you agree or disagree with your partner? Discuss your responses.

• Tell me what is in the Clipboard Group.

• Tell me what multitasking means.

• Explain how you move text with drag and drop.

• Explain how to copy text or pictures from one program to another.

Crossword Puzzle

Fill in the words across and down to complete the puzzle.

ACROSS

3. Part of the Home tab of the Word Ribbon that holds the Copy and Paste buttons

4. To take text that you copied and put it in a new location

7. To cancel the last thing you did

8. To change the location of text or other information

9. The place in the computer's memory where something goes after you copy it and before you paste it to a new location

10. A piece of work (such as a letter or a picture) that is saved in the computer; can also be part of a computer program

11. The effect of a change you make

12. To duplicate text in a document so you can put it in a different location

DOWN

1. A box that allows you to choose where to save a document

2. The place where something is

3. To take away or delete text or information you do not want

5. A box that appears when you want to save a document; it lets you type a document name

6. To do more than one thing at the same time

Working with Windows

WORKBOOK 10.1 Fill in the Blanks

Write the correct word or words in each blank.

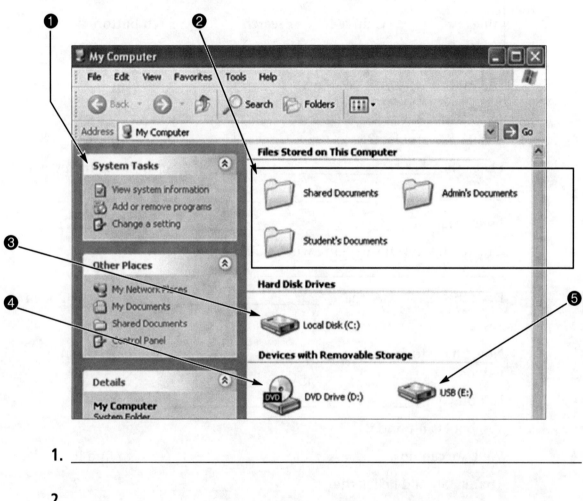

1. _____

2. _____

3. _____

4. _____

5. _____

Paired Conversation

With a partner, take turns reading the A and B parts of the conversation. Fill in each blank using the vocabulary words and computer verbs in the Word Bank.

WORD BANK

icon	double-click	choose	hourglass	program
file	C drive	search	Search button	play

Student A	Hi. You look like you need help.
Student B	Yes, I do.
Student A	What's the problem?
Student B	I click the _____, but nothing happens.
Student A	Oh. You have to _____ it.
Student B	I see! I want to _____ the Recycle Bin.
Student A	OK. You'll know it's working when you see the _____ appear.
Student B	Does that mean that the _____ will open?
Student A	Yes.
Student B	Now I have to find my _____ with my important letter.
Student A	Is it on your _____?
Student B	Yes, but I can't find it.
Student A	Well, we can do a _____ to find it.
Student B	Thanks. Should I click the _____?
Student A	No. Click the Start button and then click Search.
Student B	We can _____ music while we wait.
Student A	That's a great idea.

Vocabulary Worksheet

Fill in the blanks. Select the best answer for each sentence using the vocabulary words in the Word Bank.

WORD BANK

folder	C drive	hard drive
Search button	PrintScreen key	hourglass

1. The button that you click to start searching for a file on the computer is called the _____.

2. A _____ is a place where you can organize and keep computer files.

3. A key on the keyboard you can press to take a picture of the screen and put a copy on the Clipboard is called the _____.

4. The _____ holds all of the computer programs, including Windows. The information stays on the drive even when the computer is turned off.

5. The symbol that may appear while the computer is working on a command is called the _____.

6. The _____ is a permanent hard drive inside the computer that holds the software that makes your computer work. It can hold your files, too.

Verb Worksheet

Fill in the blanks. Select the best answer for each sentence using the computer verbs in the Word Bank.

WORD BANK

double-click	play	sort
modify	Search	choose
view		

1. To _____ means to make a small change to something in order to improve it.

2. To put things in a certain place or group according to name, size, or date is to _____.

3. To _____ means to quickly press and release the left mouse button twice.

4. To _____ means to select something from a group of different things.

5. A program feature that lets you look for something in your computer files is called _____.

6. To _____ means to look at something.

7. To _____ means to listen to a music file or to watch a video file.

Identify and Fill in the Blanks

Write the correct word or words in each blank.

1. This icon [icon] tells you that the file will open in

_____ or in one of the older versions of

_____ .

2. A file with this icon [icon] will open in _____

or another graphics program.

3. This icon [icon] tells you that the file was made in

_____ .

4. Files with this icon [icon] will open in _____ .

They are sound, music, or _____ files.

5. This is called the

_____ .

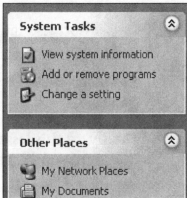

Partner Activity: Practice Reading and Pronunciation

Your teacher will read the paragraphs below as you listen to the pronunciation. Then, with a partner, take turns reading the paragraphs for one minute. The listening partner will circle words that the reader needs to practice pronouncing. Alternate reading, and listening and circling words with your partner. If you get to the end of the paragraphs before the minute ends, begin reading at the beginning. Each partner should practice reading two or three times. Ask your teacher for assistance, as needed.

PRACTICE READING

Working in My Computer is very interesting because you can learn a lot about the computer and things that you can do. Windows computers have many places to save information. To see those different places, you can look in My Computer. In My Computer, you can see the places where files can be saved. You can also open those places to see what files are there. When My Computer opens, you will see all the places to save files.

In this lesson you learned about the hard drive, the C drive, the Search button, the hourglass, and the PrintScreen key, and you learned how to double-click. In My Computer and on the Windows Desktop, you can double-click with the mouse to open choices. You always use the left mouse button to double-click. To double-click, you press and release the left mouse button twice and very quickly. When you double-click successfully, you will see the hourglass. Then a window should open and show you what you are looking for.

This lesson also taught you how to look at and understand the task pane. It is on the left side of the My Computer window. It gives you choices of common places to go on the computer. You do not have to double-click to use the task pane.

Finally, in this lesson you learned how to look for files. Sometimes you may forget the name of a file you saved or where you saved it. Windows comes with a feature called Search that helps you find files. You can search by filename or by file type. You can also go to advanced features to search by date (when it was modified) or by file size.

What I Have Learned

Take some time to think about what you have learned in Lesson 10. With a partner, take turns asking each other the questions in Exercise A and discussing the topics in Exercise B below.

EXERCISE A

Ask your partner the questions below. Begin each question with "Can you…." Your partner's answer should either be "Yes, I can" or "No, I can't." Circle the answer that your partner provides.

"Can you..."		
• Open and use My Computer?	Yes	No
• Double-click the left mouse button?	Yes	No
• Find and click the Back button?	Yes	No
• View files in different ways?	Yes	No
• Search for a file?	Yes	No
• Read and use the task pane?	Yes	No
• Insert a USB drive into the USB port?	Yes	No
• Sort files in order by size?	Yes	No

When both you and your partner have finished asking and answering the questions, look at the "No" answers on your sheet. Study and practice your book some more. Continue asking each other these questions until both of you can answer "Yes" to all the questions.

EXERCISE B

Talk about the topics below with your partner. Do you agree or disagree with your partner? Discuss your responses.

• Tell me your favorite way to view files.

• Explain how to use a USB drive.

• Describe how to use the PrintScreen key.

• Define a folder.

• Tell me how to search for music.

Crossword Puzzle

Fill in the words across and down to complete the puzzle.

ACROSS

4. This holds all of the computer programs, including Windows; information stays here even when the computer is turned off

9. A place where you can organize and keep computer files

10. A button you click to start searching for a file on the computer

11. To select something from a group of different things

12. A permanent hard drive inside the computer that holds the software that makes your computer work; it can hold your files, too

13. To make a small change to something in order to improve it

DOWN

1. A program feature that lets you look for something in your computer files

2. To look at something

3. A key on the keyboard you can press to take a picture of the screen and put a copy of it on the Clipboard

5. The symbol that may appear while the computer is working on a command

6. To quickly press and release the left mouse button twice

7. To put things in a certain place or group according to name, size, or date

8. To listen to a music file or to watch a video file